WOLVES AND PEOPLE

Wolves Discovery Library

Lynn M. Stone

The Rourke Book Company, Inc.
Vero Beach, Florida 32964

PHOTO CREDITS
© Lynn M. Stone: cover, title page, p. 4, 8, 9, 11,
15, 19, 21;
© L. David Mech: p.16; Victoria Hurst: p.12;
© Rolph Peterson: p.13

EDITORIAL SERVICES
Penworthy Learning Systems

Library of Congress Cataloging-in-Publication Data

Stone, Lynn M.
    Wolves and people / Lynn Stone.
        p. cm. — (Wolves discovery library)
    Summary: Discusses the reasons that wolves were feared by some humans
and how these feelings have changed.
    ISBN 1-55916-242-2
    1. Wolves—Juvenile literature. 2. Human-animal relationships—Juvenile
literature. [1. Wolves. 2. Human-animal relationships.] I. Title.

QL737.C22 S767 2000
599.773—dc21
                                                    00-020873

Printed in the USA

CONTENTS

WOLVES AND PEOPLE

Wolves and people have shared this planet for thousands of years. In the northern half of the world, wolves once lived almost everywhere people lived. For the most part, people and wolves got along. In fact, people took wolves from the wild and tamed them. Wolves were the first tame dogs!

When human **cultures** turned to farming instead of hunting, wolves were seen as a problem. In Europe especially, people viewed wolves as fearsome and evil.

A girl makes a pal of a captive wolf pup. If hand-raised from birth, wolves can be loyal, friendly, and affectionate to their master.

5

Hand-raised wolves are not as tame as dogs. They remain wild animals. A captive wolf is far more likely than a wild wolf to bite or attack a person.

There were many wolf stories that frightened people. Remember *Little Red Riding Hood* and *The Three Little Pigs*, or *Peter and the Wolf*? In some parts of Europe people believed in fierce half-man, half-wolf creatures called **werewolves**.

The fearsome stories about wolves were **myths**, or often-told tall tales. But Europeans were afraid of wolves. Wolves, they falsely believed, would attack them. A more real belief was that wolves would attack farm animals. As people killed off wolves' prey, such as deer, wolves did kill farm animals.

Europeans killed wolves whenever they could. Wolves were wiped out of England and Ireland before 1900. By the early 1900s, wolves were gone from nearly all of western Europe.

Like dogs, hand-raised wolves enjoy hands-on attention. This wolf's lowered tail shows respect to his human owner.

Native Americans had good feelings toward wolves.
European settlers in North America destroyed as many
wolves as they could.

WOLVES AND PEOPLE IN NORTH AMERICA

The first white settlers in North America were from Europe. The Native Americans already in North America had no problem living with wolves. They respected wolves. Some Native American cultures saw wolves as their "brothers." Native Americans noted that wolves were smart, curious, and friendly toward each other. There was something humanlike about the wolf, Native Americans thought.

But Europeans who came to the New World brought their anti-wolf feelings with them. The new Americans cleared land and raised farm animals. They decided the wolves would have to go.

This lady is howling to encourage her captive wolves to howl, but wolves often prefer playing to howling.

Denali National Park, Alaska, is the best place in North America to see wild wolves. This Denali wolf pays no attention to wolf watchers.

Wolves from Ontario, Canada, crossed frozen Lake Superior one winter and settled on Isle Royale, Michigan. Here an Isle Royale pack finishes a moose kill.

13

English settlers began living in Massachusetts in 1620. By 1630, Massachusetts offered a **bounty** for wolves. A bounty is a reward given to a hunter for killing a certain animal.

For nearly 350 years, the United States was in a war against wolves. Ranchers, farmers, and other fearful people wanted wolves removed. The U.S. Government and many state governments eagerly helped. Government hunters used bullets, traps, and poisoned bait to kill wolves.

Wolves were gone from the Eastern United States before 1900. In the West, they were wiped out by the 1930s.

Many hunters wanted wolves "controlled." The hunters believed that wolves were killing too many of the animals the hunters wanted to kill.

By 1960, the only wolves in the United States were in Alaska and Minnesota, and on Isle Royale, Michigan.

Wolves in Alaska, where few people lived, were not in great danger. But Minnesota was still paying wolf bounties as late as 1965. The few wolves on Isle Royale were safe because it was a national park.

Canada has a much smaller human population than the United States. The wolves in Canada remained widespread, except in Newfoundland.

These U. S. Government scientists are studying wolves to help protect them. This wolf in Minnesota has been drugged so that it can be fitted with a radio collar.

WOLVES AND DOGS

Curiously, people seem to forget that wolves are first cousins of dogs. People first tamed wolves at least 12,000 years ago. These first dog pets probably came from small Indian, Chinese, or Eurasian wolves.

Dogs soon became "man's best friend." But wolves became an enemy. Only in the last 30 years or so has the wolf earned people's respect.

German shepherd has kept its wolflike size and looks. Many other dog breeds look very little like their wolf ancestors.

WOLVES AND PEOPLE TODAY

The wolf hasn't changed. It is still a powerful, skilled **predator**, or hunter. And its howls still cause a chill and thrill in anyone lucky enough to hear them.

It is people's feelings toward the wolf that have changed. Science has taught people that the old myths about wolves are untrue.

Today the wolf stars on T-shirts, calendars, cards, and jewelry. Now the wolf is a valued part of wild North America.

Adult male wolf greets his owner with a sloppy "kiss." Scientists have studied captive wolf packs to learn more about how wolves live.

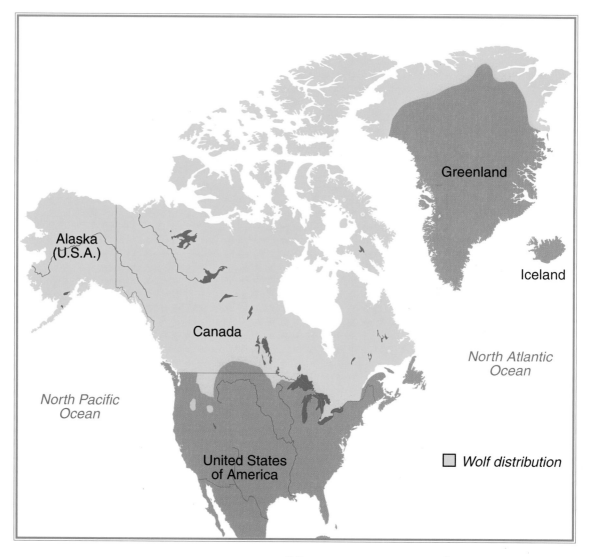

Alaska
(U.S.A.)

Canada

Greenland

Iceland

North Atlantic
Ocean

North Pacific
Ocean

United States
of America

☐ *Wolf distribution*

GLOSSARY

bounty (BOWN tee) – a reward for the killing of an animal

culture (KULL cher) – the special ways in which a certain group of people lives

myth (MITH) – an often repeated story or tale which is not true, but is often believed

predator (PRED uh ter) – an animal that hunts and kills other animals for food

prey (PRAY) – an animal that is hunted for food by another animal

werewolves (WER woolfz) – half-man, half-wolf creatures in old European tales

FURTHER INFORMATION

Find out more about wolves with these helpful books and websites:

International Wolf Center on line at www.wolf.org

Lawrence, R.D. **Wolves**. Sierra Club, 1990

Patent, Dorothy Hinshaw. **Gray Wolf Red Wolf**. Clarion, 1990

Swinburne, Stephen. **Once a Wolf**. Houghton Mifflin, 1999

INDEX

DEMCO